Francesco Maglione

CHRISTIAN ANARCHY

XERIOS

Abstract

Verses released on existential Topics.
There is no artwork if there are no content.
Content automatically generate the expression
forms.
The daily living continually puts us in front of
great existence dilemmas: where do we come
from, who are we, what is the purpose of our
existence that while flowing is bombed by
knowledge and racked by crosses.
With "Easter" was tried to underline the human
condition inserted in Christian schemes that in
a vital path enlived by the good/bad battle
emerges the final hope: the man-Lord

The absence of government as summarizing
the Greeks with the word anarchy is the social
status last conceived by man;
over thousands of years has taken different
projections.
This collection invites "to do their duty."
If everyone did their duty to the common good
without coercion of law would automatically
anarchy and if our actions would be supported
by the love we projected towards the Christian
anarchy, as evolutionary top.
Always has been invited to perform their duties
with honesty and honor, by gospel references

to fine articles of modern democratic laws such
as. Article. 54 of the Italian Constitution.
To those who think that the poems should
speak only ray of sunshine,
of white hands or whatever ephemeral,
without opening, controversy Rapisardian or
Tolstoyan memory recall that the tasks of art
there is to summarize the historical moment in
which we live, generate ideas, and if possible
solutions.

The partners

A man
A woman
In love

Eternal union
The absolute

The authentic
Otherwise
plays
the confirm
continuous
constant
of its negotiation

agonizing fears
stop

the eternal
corporeal
doesn't exist

endless growth
spiritual

relationship
daily stabbed
by stocks
deep
bleeding

and
healed
where
love is strong

MOMENTS

Supportive moment
Of binding charity

An estimated action
Looks at me
And releases

drops
of happiness

Emanation

mouths
spit out words
from their hearts
vibrations
instinct
distressful

Easter

Cross's tear
No fading
From the principalities
Doesn't rest
But pour in blood

tolerance
calm
modest
celebrates
the maximum sacrifice
accepted

after
free
pure energy

material
time
space

dominion

essence
of the being

having in hand with joy
the destiny
of the universe
Lord

When man
The brother
Won't whip
With his chains

And life
In race heritage
With solidarity

Memories

Dark
rain
tight
improvise changes

little heat
pale colors
ice

unspeakable sneer
emptiness

I tried to fly
Towards my universe
But when awake

The stars
wet
were only in the dream

Chains

When the distress
Of pent-up anxiety
Gnaws the throat
then
with the eyes
in the sordidness
also a man
can cry
and there will a day in which
no more tears
will be saw
on alienated faces
straight
with a
resigned look
towards nothing
but explosion
of rage and fury
will shout
for justice
the arrogance

broken
light
at cosmic equilibrium
and joy
vanes
for the creation

For artists

On the line
Melody in flames

music
now dust
in combustion
craving

towards wind
the fleeting black
brings back
your élan
explosive
towards all nice

the song
universal canticle
will arise

Beyond

A love beyond
time
and space

inter-dimensional

fast

Eros gives

quietly

time and space

to lovers

Shrine

Spiritual fragrance

delicate

majestic

perfume the shrine

Blood

And men
In war
And blood

poor
cut in the ghetto
by arrogance
running
towards
nothing

death

technological man
with archaic
passion

how many
red gash
on your way

Knowledge

Young man
Who grows
toughen
in the ancestral fire
interfaced
towards good and bad
fulminating
the universe you cross
towards your destiny

because of the pain
the knowledge

'900

take birth
the masses
with the media
the arrogance
amplify
the cheat
authoritarian
democratic
refined

new potentate
colored
thrown out
by the beast

specious ideals
for wars
between principalities
that dispute
the supremacy
on the multitude
in order to suck
humanity

atomic

of knowledge
on man

in the year 2000
in procession
the people
against
misuse of power
in the squares
worldwide
asking
love

Cities

Foulness patina
breathes

among the excrement
of the morning
vagabond

buzzard
perched
in the neighborhood
waiting for food

Sunday banners
satiate

manipulate
exchange souls
for sex

people rushing
all
as merchandise

work

people
together
burst to life
triumph hymns

Fog

light
fluid
involving

floats

delicate harmony
caress
calm
enchant

A baby

answer
to life questions
a baby

cries
to duty

laughs
strong
love generator

joy hymn
binding force
of the family

Bread

Good smell
Wanting to live

wheat
buckwheat
concert
under the wind
adorned with red

people support
global food
pure
body of Christ

protect
the bread
from the hand
of crime

Calvary

The soul
imploded
purified
is projected
radiant
beyond
the Calvary

Grey

Grey day
cold
empty
clipper élan
leaf in the wind
among people
with no interest
only
in the
imploding clay
two big eyes
in the window
the door
banged by wind
noise of glass
shiver
desire
of having you here with me

Outline

As a test animal
imprisoned
in a crystal bell jar
the grub
watch me
sympathize
laugh at
humiliate
hate
don't understand
who knows
enjoys the essence
the man is alive

On the road

A band
Is playing
Music is in the air
A girl dreams

The mother
Pulls her away
By an arm

Queens

soft
docile

the queens

with their walk
break
the world storyline

balance

but reflect
royal whips

Free jazz

All despair
Of human beings
Involve me

Royal monsters
bombed
from sounds
as horrendous
Chinese masks
contest
the agony
of my soul

a hand
digs
in the stomach
twirls
the intestines

the eyes
with no dreams
wide
a computer keyboard
the face

I see you already
Man coming from the future
In the despair of impotence

Failure

there

a ship
tossed around
by drain storm waves

the turned off engine
the not in gear helm
doesn't want to surrender
to the engulf
of the drain sea
that assails

on the deck
the disparate strength
of a loser

Landscape

Look
It seems
The world

Wants to keep us all
ecstatic
we contemplate
colors and graphics
transforming
material
in pulsating energy
that invades
the nothing
removing
ontological
harmonies

Politician

faces
static
cheerful
charlatan

masks

clear
lethal
indecision
real or formal
progress

runs into
the surrounding
that craves
gang ravage

Fire

loaded
point
aimed
fire
the rebellious Prometheus
meal of the Raptor
gives

feeds
heat
lights
blends

the beginning
the limb sacrificed for the
pride of a people
funerals of King

glory
pride
embodied
in the looting

cursed dragon

meat melted on the pyre
indomitable spirits
alive
clear
saints

flaming crosses
shame of race

holocaust

peoples in napalm

ink
of God
in the bath
Christian
forge

The boys
do not speak
shout

left
masters of space-time

on the streets
shout to God
compact in generation
the joy of belonging and
the thanks

of group the frenzy of doing
bully the need to be there
huge the dreams
stratospheric the events

ready to build a society
of good
to clean it

slashed

strangled
swallowed up by the dark
no more tears keep
cold words

away

unhealthy
education to respect and the
love

thrown
chained
in a bank
between knowledge deaths
object
of looting
material and spiritual
pleasure of vainglory
thirst for power unexpressed
subculture
the impulses
the joy
governed
guided
so clarifying and prim
following rules

false
inhuman
anti-Christian

authoritarian
respect
of system

the rejection

not more bricks for the new

meat tissue
couriers
buriers of dogs
a finger on the trigger
fat for masters
split unpunished
ninos de rua

pain
for dissolutions and plagues
adult

worst

                    tertiary
                   quaternary
        parasitism multifunctional
             to suck with titles
                     false
                   of work
                  the fruit

            to death the creative
         perpetual humanity sold

      one sin will not be forgiven
          one against the spirit

The girls do the sciula

The girls do
the sciula

bombs of joy

embrace the world

At least you do not expect in this hot July Sunday

light dress
the sweat
paste
carving a
the body
dominates
the woman
with naturalness of female

for such great beauty
God smiles in the Mass
refreshment
from the sea of requests

to great strides it disappears

suddenly
wide the neckline

                    bejeweled
                    generating
              fragrances amniotic

                     appears

          dragging a rattle in hand

                      mom

                    squirrels
                    cling to
                 rise to the sides
             they encircle the neck
                    kisses

                      dad

                     razor
                     hatred

                    lawyers
                    courts
                    custody

                    family
                    loses

delivery of weapons
one who divides
the make film hymn

they also want the father

Christian anarchy

hopes
ideological
killed

until
the blood
of Christian anarchy
with violence
himself
imposes

for thousands of years
he

that even before birth

all the invested
of authority of the earth
they gave the hunting to kill
him

from the slaveries
the humanity freed

the input
in his kingdom
offered
systemic perfection

guides
gave
to future
heavenly
happiness

pastors of ecclesia
which you are placing
the stick
straightens roads

instead of beating the goat
between the horns

comfortable followed it with the
whole flock

granted credit and presence
his servants
smokescreens wrap the creed
knowledge uncoordinated
contents emptied
formalisms secularized

inner seals confused

martyrdom
the Christian
Calvary
reassess
lengthening the times

theological training antitrentin
to build pastors pseudosiracides
to enslave spirits
to the consist
however
powers
to chase from the churches
The Lazarus of 2000

you pretend
God
on the stole

sort blessings and curses
According to your
command

to the generator of all freedom
loving

bend
subjugate
to your
grim passions

or
be gone
alone

priests and band
you're out

exaggerated
and
the Exasperated
not more alone
the fig tree wither
He will also deliver
will switch to the sword

poor

humble
workers
bought for a beer
seduced by false prophets
theorists nothing

good people
honest
just
place resume
in the assembly

dialectic
reported

Christ is your
witness

launched
a bridge
operating

be a friend
with the Lords of the universe
softened
the loneliness

immense the knowledge
creative
at the top evolutionary

Tatu

bodies
pierce
marked

delivered
the temple

not love kisses

soothers beast
to sucking beasts

winners
however
terrible warriors

conflict
infinite

no peace

Discotheque

air

one pair

go via the same
hand in hand
indissoluble
bunker
aura
impenetrable

intact

in their eyes
happy certainty

great sadness
for more needless sex
imagine love

Old companion

Red flag will be triumphant

parades
rallies
banners
flags
occupations
graffiti
spray

conflicts blacks
urban warfare
class in struggle

the party

great leaders
massacres

martyrdoms

clash of worlds
planned economy
to cancel profiteers and sucks
blood

needs
misery
poverty stamped
in the dream
men brothers

crumbled the wall

masters
without barriers
globalized

the small
to the power
with growl

bone in his mouth

quietly
softly entangled

satiated
bureaucratic
bearing
filter
bulwark

systemic elements

the usual generators
of misery and poverty

hopes all sell

no saints to which voted on
the idea has taken away even
those

absurd rules
democratically
subscribed

caged

blind fury
only answer

international future humanity

I asked my Father

covered with signs
I asked my father

return it to the sender
with the interests

my every word
action
overturned
opinion
public slander

I want to shake the dust
take back the peace

he told me
not curse them
forgive them

I forgive the offenses
not the actions
against humanity

are back
sodomy and gomorra
will be destroyed

Bless the work
with a gesture
it showed the fruits

he saw my chains
smiling
showed me the pieces

I still feel the weight
stuck
took me by the hand

I'm walking
I can run
torturers
now only crowds of people
when I passed

SCRIBE

intellectual
sensitive humanity
swelling of culture
masters of the word
Scientists of communication
scourges of deviance
informative
with the risk
coordinate of the facts the why
trace solutions
nothing without the consultant

scribblers

in the first row
always
to flattering the powerful
conceal
justify
defend
the work
you are eating of leftovers

burning hooked
do not teach

                lost hope
        people without light
        knowledge subservient
                first
            will massacre

            the knowledge
        has only one master
        the common good
            do your duty

Born free

Cannibalism

Give us the law
is within you

nobody respects it
I'm afraid
I want a king

not subject yourself

I can not
to control the evil

the king makes you a slave

if you bless
will be subject
but protected from hunger and
blade

crazy

the bad habits
dominates
no demon can oppress you

the king
is lawless
absolutist power
endless arrogance
his stuff

we want the democracy

constitution

how many deaths
unnecessary
rules helpless
consensus generated
to plunder
unpunished
just laughed
evil masters of the field

chaos

I cannot adjust to
I do not know where to start

a dictator
order and respect

puppet
head down to the stick

Give me a king
will never be good

I had done free

you know the crime
not love it
not reverence it
in the teeth, get a kick

the wise, you know
give to him strength
will work for you

when the seals moral
breath of life
will become

automatically
the harmony

Supreme Love

supreme love
for knowledge
shared evils
gives

Index

25. Politician
26. Fire
27. The guys do not talk, scream
28. The girls make the sciula
29. As you least expect it in
    this hot July Sunday
30. Christian anarchy
31. Tatu
32. Discotheque
33. Old companion
34. I asked my Father
35. Scribe
36. Born free
37. Supreme love

www.ingramcontent.com/pod-product-compliance
Lightning Source LLC
LaVergne TN
LVHW021546080426
835509LV00019B/2866